The life cycle of a
Ladybird

Ruth Thomson

WAYLAND

First published in 2008 by Wayland,
a division of Hachette Children's Books

Copyright © Wayland 2008

Wayland
338 Euston Road
London NW1 3BH

Wayland Australia
Level 17/207 Kent Street
Sydney, NSW 2000

Editor: Clare Lewis
Designer: Simon Morse
Consultant: Michael Scott OBE, B.Sc

Photographs: Cover (tr), 10 blickwinkel/Alamy; Cover
(main), 6 blickwinkel/Kottmann/Alamy; Cover (br), 1, 15, 23
(br) Andrew Darrington/ Alamy; 2 Redmond Durrell/Alamy;
11 Holt Studios International Ltd/Alamy; 8 Juniors
Bildarchiv/Alamy; 12 Mercer/insects/Alamy;
17 Papilio/Alamy; 7 WoodyStock/Alamy; 3, 4,
5, 6, 8, 9, 13, 14, 16, 18, 19, 20, 21, 22, 23 naturepl.com

British Library Cataloguing in Publication Data
Thomson, Ruth
    The life cycle of a ladybird. - (Learning about
    life cycles)
    1. Ladybugs - Life cycles - Juvenile literature
    I. Title
    595.7'69
ISBN-13: 978-0-7502-5598-1

Printed and bound in China

Wayland is a division of Hachette Children's
Books, an Hachette Livre UK company
www.waylandbooks.co.uk

Contents

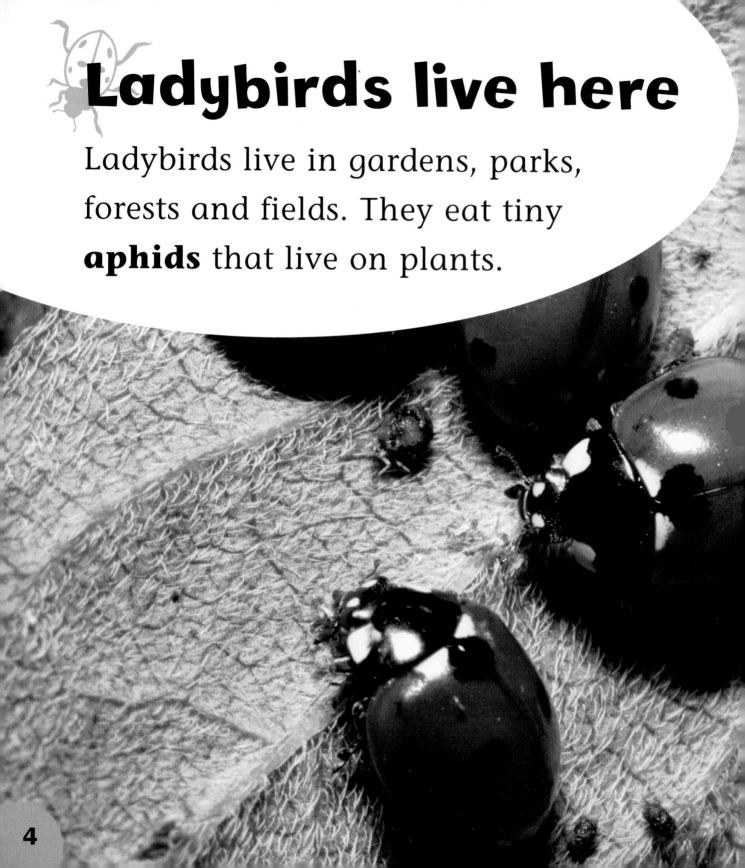

Ladybirds live here

Ladybirds live in gardens, parks, forests and fields. They eat tiny **aphids** that live on plants.

What is a ladybird?

A ladybird is an **insect** with a hard skin that protects it. Its bright colour and spots warn birds that it tastes nasty.

A seven-spotted ladybird ▼

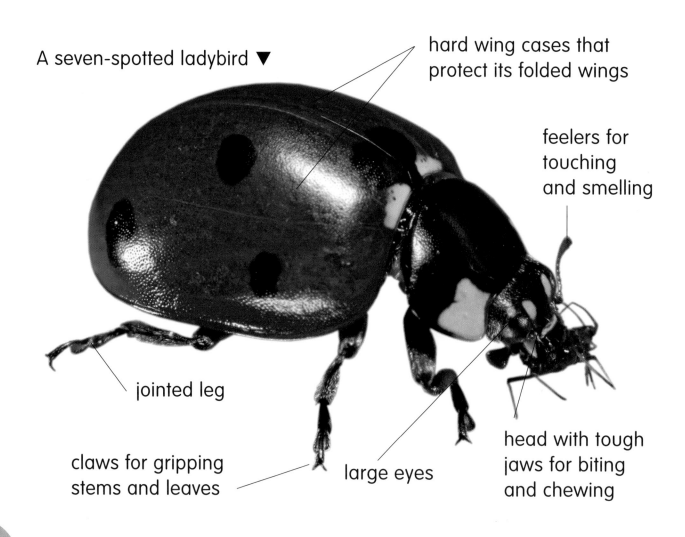

hard wing cases that protect its folded wings

feelers for touching and smelling

jointed leg

claws for gripping stems and leaves

large eyes

head with tough jaws for biting and chewing

wings

When a ladybird flies, it lifts
its spotty wing cases and fans
out large see-through wings.

Time to lay eggs

In spring, the male ladybird looks for a female. He finds her by her special smell. The ladybirds **mate**.

A week later, the female lays lots of sticky eggs. She lays them in groups on plants where **aphids** live.

9

Hatching

After a few days, a tiny **larva** **hatches** from each egg. At first, it is white. Soon it turns black.

The larva feeds on **aphids**.
It is hungry all the time.
As the larva grows bigger,
its skin becomes too tight.

1 week

Moulting

The tight skin splits and comes off. This is called **moulting**. The **larva** has new skin underneath. It moults three more times as it grows.

The larva eats about 30 **aphids** a day. It sucks the juices out of them through its hollow tongue. The larva grows even bigger.

2-3
weeks

Pupa

The fat **larva** stops eating. It fixes its tail to a stem with sticky glue. Its skin splits for the last time. There is a **pupa** inside.

3-4 weeks

The pupa hangs completely still.
Inside its hard case, the pupa
changes into an adult ladybird.

Adult ladybird

Soon the ladybird is ready
to come out. It pushes
itself head first out of the case.
Its body is soft, pale and damp.

5
weeks

The ladybird rests until its body hardens. It opens its wings so that they dry out. Soon its spots and red colour appear.

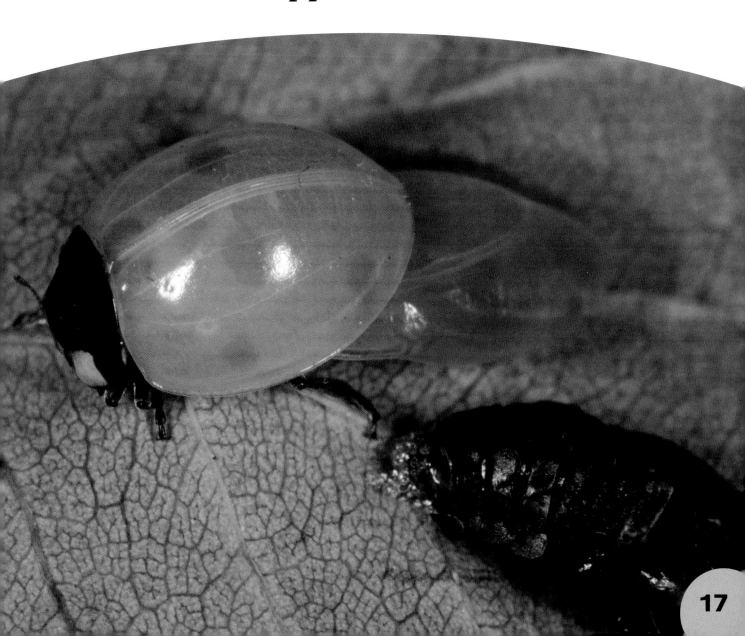

Feeding

The ladybird flies from plant to plant all summer eating **aphids**.

The ladybird also sips **nectar** from flowers. The nectar gives it energy for flying.

Sleeping through winter

When the weather turns colder, there are fewer **aphids** around. Ladybirds crowd together in a sheltered place. They sleep there all winter.

Ready to mate

In spring, when the weather warms up,
the ladybird wakes up. It flies away
to look for food and to **mate**.
The female will lay new eggs.

Ladybird life cycle

Eggs
In spring, the ladybird lays eggs in groups of 10 to 50 on leaves.

Larva
The **larva** hatches and eats **aphids** for three to four weeks.

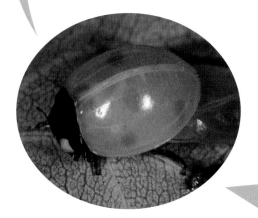

Adult ladybird
After a week, an adult ladybird comes out of the pupa.

Pupa
The larva becomes a **pupa**.

Glossary

aphid a tiny insect, such as greenfly and blackfly, that feeds on plants

hatch to come out of an egg

insect a small creature with six legs, a three-part body – head, thorax and abdomen – and a pair of feelers

larva an insect in its first stage after coming out of an egg

mate when a male and female join together to produce young

moulting shedding skin (or hair or feathers)

nectar the sweet liquid inside many flowers

pupa the form that an insect takes when it changes from a larva into an adult

Index